The Cat in the Hat's Learning Library

The Cat in the Hat's Learning Library

The Cat in the Hat's Learning Library

The Cat in the Hat's Learning Library

The Cat in the Hat's Learning Library

The Cat in the Hat's Learning Library

The Cat in the Hat's Learning Library

The Cat in the Hat's Learning Library

The Cat in the Hat's Learning Library

The Cat in the Hat's Learning Library

The Cat in the Hat's Learning Library

The Cat in the Hat's Learning Library

The Cat in the Hat's Learning Library

The Cat in the Hat's Learning Library

For Mike, my favorite mammal
—C.B.C.

The editors would like to thank
JIM BREHENY
Director, Bronx Zoo,
for his assistance in the preparation of this book.

Visit us on the Web!
Seussville.com
rhcbooks.com

Educators and librarians, for a variety of teaching tools, visit us at RHTeachersLibrarians.com

Library of Congress Cataloging-in-Publication Data is available upon request.
ISBN 978-0-525-58164-2 (trade) — ISBN 978-0-525-58165-9 (lib. bdg.)

MANUFACTURED IN CHINA
10 9 8 7 6 5 4 3 2 1
First Edition

The Cat in the Hat's Learning Library

SUPER-DEE-DOOPER BOOK OF ANIMAL FACTS

by Courtney Carbone

Random House New York

CONTENTS

Introduction

Hello, dear reader.
I'm the Cat in the Hat.
I've come here to tell you
all about this and that.

We'll learn about animals
that can swim, jump, and fly.
Please step up and join me—
there's no need to be shy!

We'll get some help learning
from Thing Two and Thing One.
We'll be animal experts
by the time we are done!

What do all the animals on Earth have in common?

Each one makes its home in a habitat. A habitat is the place where an animal lives. It provides animals with all they need.

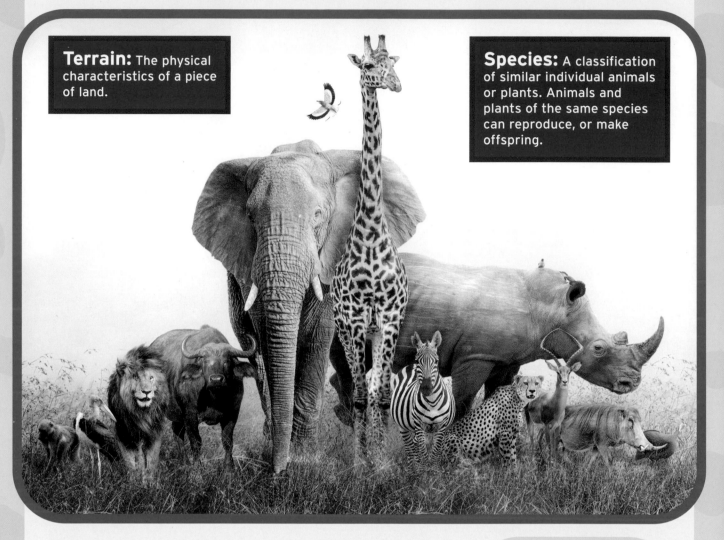

Terrain: The physical characteristics of a piece of land.

Species: A classification of similar individual animals or plants. Animals and plants of the same species can reproduce, or make offspring.

There are many different types of habitats. The type of terrain, climate, and amount of rainfall each landscape gets varies from place to place. For example, deserts, forests, mountains, grasslands, and rain forests are all very different places where animals make their homes.

Habitats are home to many different species of animals. That's because animals live in ecosystems. An ecosystem is a group of animals and plants that live together as a community. In an ecosystem, every creature—from the smallest insect to the largest predator—has an important role.

BASIC NEEDS:
- Air
- Water
- Food
- Shelter

Habitat vs. Ecosystem

Looking at a pond is a good way to learn the difference between a habitat and an ecosystem. Many animals, such as fish and insects, make their home in a pond. The pond is the habitat in which they live. It provides them with water, food, and shelter. But this pond habitat also contains an entire ecosystem! The ecosystem is how all the animals that live in the pond relate to one another and form a community. They depend on each other, as well as on the plants and nonliving things in their environment, to work together for survival.

Animals that share an ecosystem aren't necessarily friends, though. A tadpole nibbling on algae is food for a dragonfly. A dragonfly is food for a pike. A pike is food for a heron. When a heron dies and its body decays, nutrients enter the soil and water which help grow plants like algae. Then everything starts again. This is how the food chain works. It's pretty perfect, don't you think?

This book is organized by types of animals and where they make their homes. Read on to learn more about different continents, countries, climates, ecosystems, and habitats. Feel free to read the book from beginning to end or just skip around to the parts that interest you most!

AFRICAN ANIMALS

Africa is the second-largest continent in the world (after Asia). It is made up of forty-eight different countries on the mainland, plus six island nations. Africa is home to some of the world's most well-known animals.

Africa can sustain a wide variety of animals, including over 1,100 species of mammals!

ZEBRAS are famous for their striped coats. When a baby zebra is born, it has brown stripes. The stripes turn black as it ages. Zebras' stripes help them confuse predators, like lions. When zebras stand together, it's hard to see where one begins and another ends.

Even though zebras look similar, each has its own unique stripe pattern. Just like no two human fingerprints are the same!

GIRAFFES are the tallest animals in the world. A male giraffe can stand almost 19 feet tall. They feed on the leaves of tall trees. Their black tongues can measure over a foot and a half long!

Baby giraffes are called calves. Even with their long, lanky legs, calves are able to stand up within half an hour of being born.

Kindergarten:
A group of young giraffes that are watched over by one female giraffe. (Kind of like a babysitter!) Mother giraffes take turns doing this job.

AFRICAN ELEPHANTS can grow over 10 feet tall and weigh 7 tons! They're the largest land animals in the world. They live in herds, which are groups of family members led by the oldest female. Elephants can live to be seventy years old!

An elephant's trunk is made entirely of muscle. It's used for breathing, smelling, making sounds, grasping, and lifting objects. When elephants meet each other, they sometimes shake trunks just like humans would shake hands.

During the dry season, animals flock to natural and human-made water holes to drink and cool off. African buffalo, **WARTHOGS**, and hippopotamuses are some of the animals that like to swim in water to escape the heat.

Just like humans, **HIPPOPOTAMUSES** have skin that can get sunburned. Instead of sunscreen, hippos use mud to protect their skin.

Two different types, or species, of **RHINOCEROSES** are found in Africa: the white rhino and the black rhino. White rhinos graze on grass while black rhinos mostly browse leaves from shrubs and low tree branches. They also aren't really black or white, just different shades of gray!

Small birds called oxpeckers clean ticks off a rhino's hide. The oxpecker gets a good meal, and the rhino gets rid of itchy ticks!

BIG CATS

Africa is home to three of the largest cats in the world—the lion, the cheetah, and the leopard—but it is also home to seven other species of wild cats. Lions, cheetahs, and leopards make their home on the African savannas.

Savanna: A geographical region characterized by hot, grassy plains.

A difference between large cats and small cats (like the ones people keep as pets) is that small cats purr and most big cats **ROAR**!

LIONS live in groups called prides. While they are ferocious when awake, lions actually sleep much of the day!

AFRICAN ANIMALS

Cubs:
The young of certain animals, such as lions, tigers, and bears.

When the time is right, a pregnant lioness leaves her pride and finds a hidden place, like a cave or a thicket of grass, to give birth. This helps protect the cubs—that are born blind and helpless—from predators.

Lion cubs are born with brown spots that disappear after three months.

LEOPARDS are cats with black spots in neat sets of circular patterns called rosettes. These cats sleep during the day and hunt at night. Leopards are strong swimmers and good at climbing trees. That's where they spend a lot of their time!

Extend: To push out.

Retract: To pull in.

Cats, like leopards, scratch at things to keep their claws clean and sharp. Most cats can extend and retract their claws. When they retract, the claws go into pockets of skin called sheaths.

Cheetahs can purr, but they can't roar!

CHEETAHS are spotted cats that can run up to seventy miles per hour! In fact, they can reach these speeds in just a few seconds. That's faster than a sports car! When cheetahs run, they grip the ground with their claws so they don't slip. Unlike many cats, cheetahs have claws that do not retract.

Foul ball! Cheetah cubs sometimes play with elephant poop like it's a ball.

SLITHERY SNAKES!

Africa is home to many different types of snakes, including cobras, vipers, and mambas. Some of these cold-blooded reptiles are harmless, but others are extremely dangerous—even deadly! That's because the bite of some snakes contains venom.

Venom: The poison in some snakes (and other animals) that is passed on to prey through a bite or a sting.

Snakes can have stripes, spots, or rings on their skin. These markings help them blend in with their surroundings.

Snakes' jaws are loosely attached on each side of their mouth. This allows them to open very wide to swallow prey.

Q. How does a snake smell?

A. With its tongue! The tongue picks up scent molecules from the air.

ROCK PYTHON

Snakes with a venomous bite, like cobras, have special teeth called fangs.

ROCK PYTHONS kill their prey by squeezing and suffocating them. For this reason, they're called constrictors.

CARPET VIPERS are small but very dangerous snakes. Their brown or gray coloring allows them to stay hidden in grass and rocks, where they wait for unsuspecting prey.

Fangs: Teeth that are hollow for the purpose of injecting venom.

CARPET VIPER

ALL ABOUT ANTELOPE

Most species of antelope live in Africa, though some are also found in Asia. To avoid predators, antelope travel in big groups called herds. All male and most female antelope have horns, which they can use to fight off predators—and sometimes other antelope!

GIANT ELANDS are the largest antelope in the world.

ROYAL ANTELOPE are only 10 inches tall!

SICKLE-HORNED SABLES are shy antelope with soft coats.

Sickle: A tool used for cutting that has a curved metal blade.

IMPALAS are smaller antelope. They can be identified by the stripes on their backsides that look like the letter *M*.

HYENAS are the natural predator of antelope. They also eat animals that are dead or dying. For this reason, they are known as scavengers.

GREATER KUDU antelope have curved horns.

PRIMATES

Primates are mammals that have forward-facing eyes and hands that can grasp things. Examples of primates are monkeys, apes, lemurs, lorises, tarsiers, and humans!

The three main groups of primates are:

M = MONKEYS
A = APES
P = PROSIMIANS

Memory trick:
The first letter in each of the three primate groups spells out MAP!

Mammals:
Warm-blooded animals that (with a few exceptions) give birth to live young, produce milk to feed them, and have hair.

WHAT'S THE DIFFERENCE BETWEEN MONKEYS, APES, AND PROSIMIANS?

Scientists use many different—often complex—ways of classifying monkeys, apes, and prosimians. But there are also some easy ways to tell the difference. For example, monkeys have tails, but apes do not. Apes also tend to be larger and have more highly developed brains. Prosimians, on the other hand, are the most primitive of the primates. Prosimians are generally nocturnal, unlike most monkeys and apes.

Nocturnal: Active by night.

YOU SAY IT!
Prosimians = pro-SIM-ee-unz

DID YOU KNOW?
HUMANS are primates, too. That's right—you're a primate! You may even be able to hang from your arms and legs.

PRIMATES

MONKEYING AROUND

Most monkeys can leap through the air and jump from tree to tree using their arms, legs, and tails. Many monkeys have prehensile tails that can grasp like a hand. One exception to this is the baboon, which does not have this kind of tail and spends most of its time on the ground.

Prehensile:
Capable of grasping.

BABOONS live and travel together in large groups called troops. They walk on all fours. Baboons are omnivores with sharp teeth. They enjoy grooming and spend many hours picking bugs out of each other's fur.

Omnivore:
An animal that eats meat and plants.

BABOONS like to sleep in high places to avoid predators. If you've ever been worried about falling out of a bunk bed, baboon life is probably not for you.

MANDRILLS are the largest monkeys of all. They have golden beards and red and blue faces. The males are larger and more colorful than the females.

AMAZING APES

Apes have broad chests and strong arms. Some, like **GORILLAS** and chimpanzees, use their arms to help them get around by walking on their knuckles.

Apes are noisy! Day and night, they shriek, squeak, whistle, whoop, and grunt.

Gorillas are the largest apes in the world.

Gorillas walk around on all fours. They eat mostly plants. Depending on their size and sex, gorillas can eat 20 to 40 pounds of ripe fruit, as well as flowers, leaves, stems, and bamboo shoots per day.

Mother gorillas build nests made of branches and leaves. They look like a birds' nest—only a LOT bigger!

BONOBOS are apes, but they are smaller than chimpanzees and gorillas. They have a light red mouth, and hair parted on either side of their head.

Bonobos eat termites. Sometimes they use sticks as tools to pull the termites out of the ground.

CHIMPANZEES, sometimes called chimps, are covered with brown or black hair, except for their palms, ears, and face. They are larger than bonobos but smaller than gorillas.

Chimps can smile, frown, and laugh—just like us! They also show signs of affection—like hugs, kisses, and pats on the back!

Chimps can see colors! This helps them pick ripe yellow bananas instead of less tasty green ones.

Like bonobos, chimpanzees sometimes use tools. For example, they may use a stick to get honey from bee hives.

PLAYFUL PROSIMIANS

Prosimians, like lemurs, lorises, and tarsiers, are the most primitive form of primates.

Some smaller prosimians live in trees, but larger prosimians tend to live on the ground. They are mostly nocturnal animals.

The word *prosimian* comes from *pro,* which means "before," and *simi,* which means "monkey" or "ape."

GALAGOS have large pointy ears, round eyes, and a round head.

Galagos are also called bush babies because the noises they make sound like human babies crying.

LEAPIN' LEMURS!

LEMURS are prosimians that are only found in one place on Earth: the island of Madagascar. There are over a hundred different species of lemur, but some species arc made up of just a few individuals. They are considered one of the most endangered animals on Earth.

Madagascar is an island off the coast of Africa. It is home to many unique and fascinating animals. In fact, many animals live in Madagascar and nowhere else!

33

Arboreal:
Living in or traveling through trees.

MONGOOSE LEMURS are arboreal.

RING-TAILED LEMURS spend a lot of time on the ground. Their tails are covered in black-and-white rings, which gives them their name.

YOU SAY IT!
Arboreal =
ar-BOR-ee-ul

MADAME BERTHE'S MOUSE LEMURS are the smallest lemurs of all. Each one is about the size of a thumb!

AYE-AYES have bright orange eyes and dark brown or black fur tipped with white. They also have sharp claws.

Aye-ayes are nocturnal lemurs. Their big ears help them find food in the dark. They can even hear tasty bugs moving under tree bark!

35

AMERICAN ICONS

From seashores to mountain ranges to wide-open prairies, the habitats found throughout the United States are as varied and diverse as the animals that live in them. Some of these animals have become symbols of our country.

The **BALD EAGLE** is the national bird of the United States of America. To Americans, this bird is a symbol of freedom. Eagles soar through the air on their majestic wings.

Bald eagles are not bald! Their heads are covered with white feathers.

Symbol:
Something that stands for something else.

36

You've probably seen pictures of **WOLVES** howling at the moon. The real reason that wolves howl is to communicate with each other. Wolves howl to let other wolves know their position, to warn about danger, and to express emotions.

Do you know the difference between **MOUNTAIN LIONS** and **COUGARS**, or **PUMAS** and **PANTHERS**? Trick question! Mountain lions, cougars, pumas, and panthers are ALL names for the same animal!

MUSTANGS are wild horses found in grassland areas of the American West. They can also be found on some islands off the Atlantic coast. They are descendants, or relatives, of escaped domesticated horses.

Domesticated:
Tamed, meaning that an animal is comfortable with people.

ALLIGATOR OR CROCODILE?

AMERICAN CROCODILES mostly live in and around ponds and creeks in swampy parts of southern Florida. They are shy creatures that like to sun themselves with their mouths open. (It helps keep them cool.)

AMERICAN ALLIGATORS are the largest reptiles in the United States. The largest one on record was 14 feet 3 inches long and weighed 899 pounds! To sneak up on prey, they keep most of their body below water. This makes them look like floating logs. But they don't look like logs when they attack!

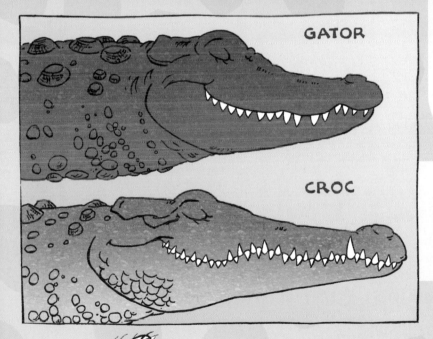

GATOR

CROC

Alligators and crocodiles look alike because they are part of the same family. But there are ways to tell them apart. (Not that you should get close enough to see the difference!)

TEETH: An alligator's upper teeth hang over its lower jaw, while a crocodile's upper and lower teeth interlock.

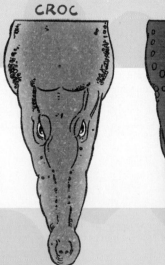

CROC   GATOR

SNOUT SHAPE: If you look at both of their heads, you'll see that a croc's snout is thin, and a gator's snout is wider.

ANTARCTIC ANIMALS

Antarctica is Earth's southernmost continent. It is the coldest, windiest, and driest place in the world and is almost completely covered with ice. The average winter temperature is 76 degrees Fahrenheit below zero. The only plants that grow here are some mosses, lichen, and algae. Nevertheless, there is a lot of wildlife!

In Antarctica, there are valleys and steep mountains buried in ice almost 2 miles deep!

A penguin is a flightless waterbird. Almost all penguins live in the southern hemisphere. The one exception, the **GALAPAGOS PENGUIN**, lives near the equator. Most penguins eat fish and krill—tiny shrimplike sea creatures.

PENGUINS waddle or hop when they walk on land. They'll sometimes slide on their bellies down hills. Penguins move fastest in the water and are excellent swimmers.

Penguins use a form of camouflage known as countershading. When swimming in the ocean, they blend in with their surroundings, making them hard for predators to spot.

If a **LEOPARD SEAL** looks down into the water, a penguin's dark back will blend in with the water's depth.

If a **KILLER WHALE** looks up from below, a penguin's white belly blends in with the ice or sky.

Camouflage:
A way that animals and plants are disguised for self-protection.

41

EMPEROR PENGUINS are the largest of all penguins.

When an emperor penguin mother lays an egg, there's nothing to build a warm nest with. Instead, the egg goes on top of the father penguin's warm feet! Until the egg hatches about sixty-five days later, the father penguin can't move, swim, or even eat!

Penguins raise their chicks together in a crèche.
They huddle to stay warm in the freezing cold!

Crèche: A large group of baby
animals being cared for by adults;
from a French word that means "crib."

CHINSTRAP PENGUINS are the most numerous of all penguins. They live in large groups and have a shrill call.

Despite their small size, **ROCKHOPPER PENGUINS** are plucky and quick to defend themselves.

GENTOO PENGUINS have a head stripe. They are also the fastest swimmers!

ADÉLIE PENGUINS live in large colonies. They watch over their eggs in rock-lined nests.

ARCTIC ANIMALS

The Arctic is the northernmost place on Earth. Believe it or not, the Arctic is not land—it is a sea of ice floating in the Arctic Ocean, surrounded by land. Imagine a circle around the top of the world. That's the Arctic Circle. It includes the Arctic Ocean and parts of Canada, Russia, Greenland, Norway, Sweden, Finland, and the United States (Alaska). The Arctic is very cold—the average winter temperature is 40 degrees Fahrenheit below zero! Animals here need special adaptations to survive the cold.

Adaptation:
A change of form or behavior to survive in different surroundings.

BLUBBER

PACIFIC OCEAN

ASIA

ARCTIC OCEAN

NORTH POLE

NORTH AMERICA

EUROPE

ATLANTIC OCEAN

AFRICA

THING 1

POLAR BEARS, seals, whales, and walruses have thick layers of blubber that keep them warm.

Polar bears' fur looks white, but it is actually colorless. They have black skin and hollow hairs that absorb the sun's rays and hold in the heat.

POLAR BEAR HAIR

FUR
SKIN
BLUBBER

Polar bears are born in a den underneath the snow. Cubs are carefully protected by their mothers, especially from adult males that might kill them if they're left unprotected.

Den: The home or shelter of a wild animal.

Polar bears have wide feet, like snowshoes. Fur on the soles of their feet keeps them from slipping on ice and snow.

An **ARCTIC FOX'S** white coat helps it hide in the snow from predators—like polar bears!

SNOWY OWLS stay warm in their feathered snowsuits.

Shaggy **MUSK OXEN** have sturdy horns and coats of thick fur to keep them warm.

Q. What's the difference between antlers and horns?

A. Horns are permanent, while antlers fall off and regrow each year of an animal's life.

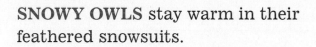

It's not always cold near the North Pole. For four months a year, there is summer!

During this time, temperatures can heat up to 80 degrees Fahrenheit.

During summer, it's sunny all day and night! That's because the North Pole is tilted toward the sun.

When it warms up, the snow begins to melt. Plants grow. Some animals, like the **ARCTIC FOX** and hare, change color from white to brown to better blend in.

CARIBOU

Migration:
The seasonal moving of a species from one place to another.

Every summer, tens of thousands of **CARIBOU** travel north to the Arctic as part of their migration pattern. On their way north, many females give birth to live young. Caribou come to graze in the warmth, then head south before bad weather arrives.

Caribou, moose, and **REINDEER** have antlers instead of horns.

REINDEER

CLIMATE CHANGE

Have you heard about climate change? Climate change refers to Earth's changing temperatures. But the temperature change is about more than just the changing of the seasons. Instead, the planet as a whole is getting warmer, which is affecting animals and people all over Earth.

Climate change: The increase in Earth's temperature in the past century, which affects the climate and the ice at the poles.

EQUATOR

ANTARCTIC CIRCLE

ARCTIC ANIMALS

One of the ways that animals are affected by climate change is by the melting of polar ice. In the Arctic, snow piles up on the land, forming ice caps and glaciers. But as temperatures rise, icebergs break off and spill into the sea. As a result, many animals are in danger of losing their natural habitats.

Scientists from all over the world are studying climate change and its harmful effects on humans and animals. They are trying to find ways to stop this from happening and to help protect people and animals.

ASIAN ANIMALS

Asia is the largest continent in the world. It is also the most populated and diverse of all the continents, with many different landscapes and regions that range from the highest peak in the world (Mount Everest) to the lowest place on land (the Dead Sea).

Wild **GIANT PANDAS** are only found in China. They live mostly in remote bamboo forests. Known for their distinct black-and-white coats, they are considered a national treasure in China.

Giant pandas eat a grass called bamboo for every meal. Can you imagine eating the same thing every single day?

Baby pandas are born blind, deaf, and with almost no hair. They are the size of a stick of butter.

NEED A HAND?

Because giant pandas are a vulnerable species, humans sometimes help them to breed and raise their young.

TIMELINE

ONE MONTH: Pandas can't do much without help.

FOUR MONTHS: Pandas begin to crawl around on their own.

SEVEN MONTHS: Pandas can now climb and eat bamboo!

CAMELS were likely domesticated thousands of years ago in the Arabian Peninsula and central Asia. These mammals are sometimes called the ships of the desert. That is because they can carry people across hot desert sands. Camels can also walk through cold, icy snow. Their wide, padded feet keep them from sinking in the sand as they walk.

ONE HUMP OR TWO?

The most common type of camel is the DROMEDARY or ARABIAN CAMEL, which has only one hump. The BACTRIAN CAMEL has two humps.

Camels can go for days— or even weeks—without drinking water!

Q. How do camels keep sand out of their nose and eyes?

A. They have nostrils that close and long, thick eyelashes!

ASIAN ANIMALS

CLOUDED LEOPARDS are wild cats native to tropical forests of Southeast Asia. They spend much of their time sleeping and hunting in trees. They have spots on their fur that look like clouds!

KOMODO DRAGONS are found only on a few Indonesian islands. They are the world's largest lizards and can grow up to 10 feet long!

Reptiles, like the Komodo dragon, are cold-blooded. This means that their temperature changes a lot. For example, they get cold when it's cold outside and hot when it's hot.

LIZARDS get warm by lying in the sun. This is called basking.

ORANGUTANS are native to the southeastern islands of Sumatra and Borneo. They love to eat fruit, like the durian. They find ripe durians in the forest and carefully peel off the rinds.

Durians have a pungent, or strong, smell. They are so stinky that, in Singapore, they are banned on public transport!

DURIAN

Orangutans have very long arms. When they stand, their hands almost touch the ground! In fact, orangutan mothers sometimes create bridges with their long arms to help their little ones get from one tree branch to another.

Adult male orangutans spend time in the trees on their own. The word *orangutan* means "person of the forest."

Native to South and Southeast Asia, **GIBBONS** are apes that spend much of their lives in trees. They swing from tree to tree using their arms. This is called brachiating, and gibbons are VERY good at it. They can actually swing up to fifty feet at a time! (That's more than the length of a typical school bus!)

Brachiating: Moving from place to place by swinging from one arm to the other.

YOU SAY IT!
Brachiating =
BRAY-kee-ate-ing

Gibbons sleep in the forks of tree branches!

YOU SAY IT!
Siamang =
SEE-uh-mang

SIAMANG GIBBONS are singing apes that live in Southeast Asia. The males have a sac of loose skin under their chins that expands to help them sing. If a female siamang is nearby, she may join the male for a duet!

Sac: A small baglike structure.

61

SNUB-NOSED MONKEYS live in forests in China and Vietnam. They travel in groups called troops. Living in groups offers monkeys protection from danger.

PROBOSCIS MONKEYS are found only on the island of Borneo. They are known for their long droopy noses, which help them to make a loud warning call. These monkeys spend most of their time in trees but are also good swimmers.

Proboscis:
A long, flexible nose.

YOU SAY IT!
Proboscis =
proh-BOSS-kuss

TARSIERS are small nocturnal primates found in tropical rain forests in Southeast Asia. They have long, slender tails and big eyes that let in lots of light. But unlike many animals, they cannot move their eyes. When tarsiers hear a sound, they have to move their whole head to look in that direction. Luckily, they can move their heads almost all the way around!

Carnivore: An animal that eats mostly meat.

Tarsiers are carnivores. They wake at sunset and forage for insects during the night. Sometimes mothers carry their babies in their mouths as they leap and climb trees!

AUSTRALIAN ANIMALS

Australia is both its own country and a continent! Much of Australia has a desert climate, but some areas, especially the eastern parts of the country, are more temperate and compatible with different types of animal life. Australia is home to many animals that are not found anywhere else in the world.

Australia is often referred to as the land Down Under. This is because it's down under the equator.

KANGAROOS, BANDICOOTS, and **WALLABIES** are a type of animal called marsupials. Most female marsupials have a pouch that they use to carry their young and to keep them safe from harm. Kangaroos, bandicoots, and wallabies are only found in Australia, New Guinea, and some nearby islands.

KANGAROO

WALLABY

BANDICOOT

Kangaroos are generally the largest of all the marsupials. They hop on their strong hind legs to get from place to place, using their tails to balance.

Joey: A young animal, usually a kangaroo.

When first born, a baby kangaroo is about the size of a red kidney bean. It's called a joey. Shortly after its birth, the joey crawls up its mother's fur and into her pouch. It will stay there for about 135 days nursing on its mother's milk.

KOALAS are another type of marsupial. Unlike kangaroos, koalas spend most of their time in trees, sleeping and eating their favorite food—eucalyptus leaves.

MONOTREMES

DUCK-BILLED PLATYPUS

ECHIDNA

Almost all mammals give birth to live young. Monotremes are mammals that lay eggs instead. There are five living species of monotreme: the **DUCK-BILLED PLATYPUS** and four different species of **ECHIDNA**. They're all native to Australia and New Guinea.

Monotreme:
A mammal that lays eggs.

Platypuses dig two burrows: a plain one for resting and one lined with leaves for nesting. Platypus mothers lay up to three eggs at a time. Each one is about the size of a (round) jelly bean. Babies can swim three to four months after hatching. They glide right into the water, ready for fun!

YOU SAY IT!
Monotremes = mah-noh-TREEMS

Burrow: A hole in the ground that an animal digs for a home or hiding place.

Snout: The nose, mouth, and upper jaw of certain animals.

Echidnas lay oval-shaped eggs that are about the size of grapes. They use an egg tooth on the end of their snout to break through their shell and hatch.

Newborn echidnas are called puggles!

ECHIDNA EGG

EGG TOOTH

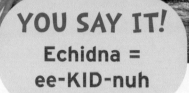

PUGGLE

NEW ZEALAND

New Zealand is a remote country, near Australia, made up of two main islands—North Island and South Island. One of the most important industries in New Zealand is sheep farming. New Zealand is also known for its kiwi birds.

Remote:
Distant or far away.

KIWI are nocturnal birds that stay out of sight during the day and search for food after dark. They can't see very well, so they use their sense of smell to hunt. Kiwi birds poke their long beaks into the ground until they sniff out something tasty, like a worm.

Kiwis are the only birds in the world with nostrils at the end of their beaks. (Most animals have nostrils up by their eyes.)

DID YOU KNOW?

Kiwi birds can't fly.

BACKYARD ANIMALS

There are all different types of backyards in the world—and in the United States! If you live in Hawaii, your backyard is probably very different from one in Alaska. And if you live in an apartment building, you might not have a backyard at all. The animals in this section, however, are creatures commonly found in much of suburban North America.

RACCOONS are common from northern South America to southern Canada. They make their home in many different habitats and can be found in many suburban areas as well as cities. Raccoons scavenge for food at night. They have human-like hands that allow them to easily get into trash cans. They eat almost anything!

Baby raccoons are called **KITS**, and they cannot see when they are born. Their mothers often hide them inside hollow trees to keep them safe while hunting for food!

Have you ever spotted a **DEER**? How about a family of deer? If so, you may have seen a baby deer, which is called a **FAWN**. Some fawns have white spots that allow them to blend into their surroundings, such as a field of flowers.

In many places, deer are being squeezed out of their natural habitat by land development. You often see them nibbling on flowers and shrubs in suburban neighborhoods.

SQUIRRELS are one of the most common animals you'll find in a suburban backyard. Tree squirrels are probably the most familiar species, but chipmunks, prairie dogs, and marmots (like the woodchuck) are also part of the squirrel family. Tree squirrels are often found in trees where they eat acorns and seeds.

RED FOXES are protective creatures. They keep their babies, also known as kits, safely hidden in a den. But if a mother fox senses danger, she'll keep moving her kits until she feels they're out of harm's way.

SKUNKS are found throughout most of North America. They're easily recognized by their black fur, white stripes, and bushy tail. A skunk's bold markings act as a warning to other animals. If someone gets too close, a skunk will stamp its feet and let loose a foul-smelling spray from its butt!

BACKYARD BIRDS

BLUE JAYS are birds found commonly throughout eastern and central North America. They eat mostly seeds, nuts, and acorns. They live in forests, parks, towns, and cities. Like their name suggests, they have bright blue feathers.

OWLS are unique, solitary birds that mostly hunt at night for prey. Owls have excellent hearing. Ear holes on the sides of their head, behind their eyes, can pick up the sound of animals moving—even underground!

Male owls make *hoo* sounds to attract female owls.

BARN OWLS are the most widespread of all owl species. They can be found on every continent except for Antarctica. Barn owls are cavity nesters. That means they make their nests and raise their young inside sheltered areas, like hollow trees, barns, church steeples, abandoned buildings, and human-made nesting boxes.

BACKYARD INSECTS

Insects are all around us. You see them every day, but how much do you know about these amazing creatures? Did you know that all insects have bodies made up of three parts: the head, the thorax, and the abdomen? They also all have six legs.

There are millions of insect species in the world!

FIREFLIES are not flies at all—they're actually beetles that light up! Each species of firefly has a different light pattern. They flash their lights at night to attract a mate.

DID YOU KNOW?

A **SPIDER** is an arachnid, **NOT** an insect. (Arachnids have two body parts and eight legs.)

Male **CRICKETS** chirp to attract mates. They do so by rubbing their wings together.

Like skunks, **LADYBUGS** give off a stinky smell when danger is near!

CATERPILLARS, BUTTERFLIES, and MOTHS

BUTTERFLY or MOTH?

Butterflies and moths are very closely related. How do you tell the difference? Butterflies generally fly during the day and are usually larger and more colorful than moths.

BUTTERFLY

MOTH

Butterflies and moths can lay hundreds of eggs at a time!

The young of butterflies and moths are called **CATERPILLARS**. Caterpillars hatch out of butterfly and moth eggs. When they first hatch, caterpillars look like tiny worms. For their first meal, most will eat their own eggshells. Then they'll eat the plant on which their eggs were laid. Caterpillars eat all the time—and quickly!

If we grew as fast as caterpillars do, in two weeks, we'd each be as big as a bus!

Caterpillars eventually grow too big for their skin. When this happens, they shed their old skin for a bigger one. Then they eat their old skin! (It is very nutritious.) Caterpillars continue to shed their skin several more times before moving on to the next stage of life.

Nutritious: Providing food necessary for life and growth.

Butterfly caterpillars hang upside down like small letter *j*s for a few hours. A shell called a chrysalis then forms around them.

UNDERWING MOTH

Throughout their time inside the chrysalis, caterpillars keep changing. When they are finally ready to break free, they will poke their tiny legs out. Now they are butterflies!

Butterflies grow inside chrysalis shells. Moths grow inside silky cocoons.

Chrysalis:
A shell that surrounds a grown caterpillar while it changes into a butterfly.

Cocoon: A silky covering that a caterpillar builds around itself before it changes into a moth.

When a butterfly first emerges from its chrysalis, its wings are too soft and wet to fly. The butterfly must wait until they harden. In the meantime, their antennae start working to sense what's around them.

Within hours, their new wings dry and harden, and they are ready to fly away!

Antennae:
A pair of long feelers on the head used to smell and feel.

WESTERN PYGMY BLUE BUTTERFLIES are the smallest butterflies in the world. Their wingspan is only about one-half inch.

The **QUEEN ALEXANDRA BIRDWING** is the largest of all butterflies. Its wingspan can reach almost a foot across!

A butterfly's wobbly flight makes it hard for birds to catch them.

The bright colors on some butterflies warn predators that they are poisonous and to stay away!

Butterflies draw nectar from flowers using a tube called a proboscis. It works just like a drinking straw!

Nectar: A sweet liquid found in many flowers.

Proboscis: In an insect, a proboscis is a tube-shaped mouth part used for sucking food or drink.

Butterflies see thousands of images at once!

DESERT ANIMALS

A desert is a place that receives very little rain. You may think of deserts as being hot and dry, but there are actually many different types of deserts. Some are freezing cold—like Antarctica, which is a polar desert! And while you may not imagine that deserts could support much life, there are actually a lot of plants and animals that live there!

Diurnal: Active by day.

HAWK

OWL

HAWKS are diurnal birds of prey. Some other desert predators, like **OWLS**, hunt at night so they don't have to compete with hawks! Being active at night helps desert animals avoid the blistering heat of the day.

The massive ears on a **FENNEC FOX** help it hear prey moving under the desert sand. Its ears also help to regulate the fennec fox's body temperature.

GECKOS are lizards with pads on their feet that are perfect for gripping. They can climb up walls—even glass ones—without falling off! There are well over a thousand different species of geckos in the world. They can be found in deserts, rain forests, and cities.

The **BANDED GECKO** is native to Texas and the American Southwest. At night, when it hunts insects, it opens its eyes wide to let in light. To protect its eyes from sunlight during the day, it keeps its eyelids almost completely shut.

Geckos got their name because some chirp and squeak, making a "geck-OH" sound.

SIDEWINDERS are rattlesnakes found in the Sonoran and Mojave Deserts in the southwestern United States. They sidewind, or move in curved S shapes, to help them travel over sandy surfaces.

TORTOISES are turtles that live on the land. They move very slowly and eat grass and other vegetation. Desert tortoises, like the ones that live in the Mojave and Sonoran Deserts, spend almost 95 percent of their lives underground. The life expectancy for these tortoises is from fifty to eighty years in the wild.

Q. What's the difference between a turtle and a tortoise?

A. Well, spelling for one! But the real answer is that turtles live in the water, and tortoises live on land.

Another animal that can be found in the desert is a **BAT**. You may have heard the phrase "as blind as a bat." The truth is bats are not blind, but some do have poor eyesight. To overcome this, they make high-pitched squeaks when they're flying. Their squeaks bounce off objects, then come back to their ears. From the sound of the echoes, they are able to tell what is around them—like tasty insects! This is a form of detection called echolocation.

Echolocation: Locating objects by making a sound that bounces off them.

Baby bats are called pups. Mother bats give birth to only one pup per year.

Some bats, lizards, and **SNAKES** are color-blind. They can only see black and gray.

Color-blind: Unable to see one or more colors.

FARM ANIMALS

What comes to mind when you hear the word *farm*? You may think of sprawling fields, livestock, and a red barn like the one in the picture. These farms are common in the United States, but they are just one of many different types of farms. Others include subsistence farms, crop farms, dairy farms, poultry farms, and fish farms. Farms can be home to a variety of animals; just one kind, such as cows or pigs; or none at all. Here are some of the animals traditionally found on farms in North America.

Subsistence farm: A farm that feeds only the people who live there.

SHEEP are raised on farms for their meat and their woolly fleece. The fleece is sheared and spun into wool to make fabric.

DID YOU KNOW?
An **ewe** is a female sheep.
A **ram** is a male sheep.
A **lamb** is a baby sheep.

COWS provide much of the milk that humans drink every day. They can be milked by hand or by milking machines.

MOO-MOOooo

chuff

chuff

TEAT CUP

CLAW

VACUUM TUBE

MILK HOSE

chuff

Not all animals are welcome on farms! **CROWS** are birds that like to eat farmers' crops. Many farmers put up scarecrows to scare hungry crows away.

In North America, **CHICKENS** are commonly found on commercial, poultry, and subsistence farms. But due to the increasing popularity of raising chickens, they are now found in suburban backyards and on city rooftops as well!

Poultry:
Domestic fowl, such as chickens, ducks, and turkeys.

It takes about twenty-one days for a chick to hatch from an egg. During that time, the yolk in the egg provides food to the growing chick. Tiny pores, or holes, in the eggshell allow air and moisture to flow in and out.

DAY 3: The chick is tiny and looks like a small letter *c*.

DAY 7: The chick is growing a beak.

DAY 12: The chick can wiggle, and bumps will begin to pop out all over its skin. These bumps will soon turn into feathers.

DAY 21: The chick is ready to hatch!

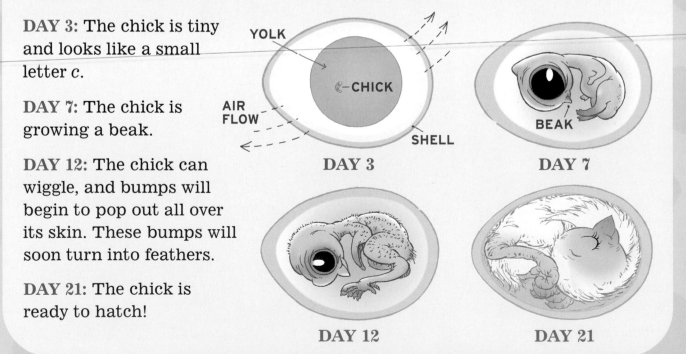

YOLK

CHICK

AIR FLOW

SHELL

DAY 3

BEAK

DAY 7

DAY 12

DAY 21

Inside the egg, baby chicks use an egg tooth on their beak to help chip their way out of their shells. This process is called pipping. Cracking open a shell is not easy. The little chicks have to work hard to finally break free. Once they hatch, chicks need to dry off before they become soft and fluffy!

Pipping: The process of breaking out of the shell of an egg.

DID YOU KNOW?

Female chickens are called **hens**.
Male chickens are called **roosters** or **cocks**.

In five or six months, the chicks will be fully-grown chickens. The females will be able to start laying eggs of their own.

Chickens like to be outside in the sunshine, with plenty of room to explore.

HORSES

Horses are helpful to humans in many ways. They can be used to plow farmland, to herd cattle, for transportation, or for sport. Some common breeds of workhorses, also called draft horses, are Belgians, **CLYDESDALES**, Percherons, and Shires.

Horses are measured in units called hands. They're only measured up to the area near their shoulder blades, which are called their withers.

A pony is a horse that's less than 14.2 hands.

One hand = 4 inches

WHICH HORSE IS WHICH?

STALLION/ SIRE

YEARLING

MARE/DAM

FOAL

A **stallion** is a male horse that is more than four years old.

A **sire** is a horse that is a father.

A **yearling** is a horse that is one year old.

A **mare** is a female horse that is more than four years old.

A **dam** is a horse that is a mother.

A **foal** is a horse that is less than one year old.

A **filly** is a female horse that is less than four years old.

A **colt** is a male horse that is less than four years old.

MORGANS are smart horses. They learn quickly how to pull carts and wagons, plow fields, herd cows, and run races.

QUARTER HORSES are a breed that started in the United States. They're easy horses to handle, and they're good at herding cows.

91

PETS

Many different domestic animals are kept as pets. In addition to dogs and cats, people keep rabbits, birds, guinea pigs, hamsters, gerbils, mice—even rats—as companions!

Owning a pet comes with a lot of responsibility. Pets need to be fed and exercised daily, and some require extensive grooming. Most require veterinary care, which can be expensive. And ALL require LOTS of attention. You need to have the time, energy, and money to take care of a pet!

If you decide to get a pet, research your choices before making a decision. Visit your local animal shelter and ask the staff for advice. You may think you want a playful kitten or puppy, but an older cat or dog that is housebroken might be a better choice.

Shelter: A place where an animal that is lost or doesn't have a home can stay.

BIRDS

There are about 10,500 known bird species in the world. Each one has feathers, two wings, two legs, one tail, and one beak (but no teeth). While large birds like parrots are beautiful to look at, they are extremely difficult to keep. And some can live for seventy-five years! Wild-caught birds should never be kept as pets, but certain types of small domesticated birds, like parakeets, cockatiels, and canaries, are friendly and make great pets.

Parakeets and canaries eat seeds and pellets, and chopped fresh vegetables and fruit.

PARAKEETS are small parrots with long pointed tails and bright feathers. They are also known as budgies. Parakeets are social and like interacting with each other. They make noises known as trills. Most parakeets live for five to fifteen years, and they're easy to care for as pets.

Trill: The rapid singing of a series of similar or alternate sounds.

Birds have three eyelids on each eye!

CANARIES are small birds that make great pets. While you probably think of canaries as songbirds, you may be surprised to learn that the males are the best singers!

GUINEA PIGS make great pets, especially if you are able to get more than one. That's because guinea pigs are social animals that like having another furry friend to keep them company. Guinea pigs exercise by climbing ramps and running through tubes.

DID YOU KNOW?

A guinea pig can live for four to eight years. Make sure you can take care of it for that long before you get one (or more) as a pet!

Guinea pig teeth are always growing. They need to have hay available at all times to grind their teeth on. In addition to hay, guinea pigs like to nibble on pellets, vegetables, and fruit.

RABBITS also make good pets. They love to explore and hop all around. Sometimes, they will play by nudging small balls across the floor. When they're not playing, rabbits like to munch on veggies, fruit, hay, and pellets. Pet rabbits usually live in special cages known as hutches. They can also be trained to use a litter box.

LOP-EARED RABBITS are popular pets. They have ears that flop over instead of standing up.

Hutch: A house for rabbits or other small animals.

DID YOU KNOW?
Rabbits usually live between eight and twelve years.

DOGS

Dogs have been living with humans since the Ice Age! Descended from wolves, dogs were the first animals to be domesticated by humans. Today, the American Kennel Club recognizes almost 200 different dog breeds, but the most common dog in America is the mixed breed, or mutt.

Dogs are carnivores, which means they eat meat. And as any dog owner can tell you, most dogs also love treats, like dog biscuits!

Dogs' tails help them balance— like a rudder on a boat!

Dogs love to play!

Breed: A group of animals having a clearly defined set of characteristics.

Dogs give birth about sixty-three days after mating. Depending on the breed, the mother can have up to thirteen puppies at a time!

Puppies like to growl and nip when they play. They also like to play-fight with each other.

Some puppies can grow to be ten times their original size!

DOG DETAILS

VISION: Dogs have good vision. Their keen sense of sight helps them see better than people when the light is dim.

HEARING: Dogs can hear high-pitched sounds that people can't hear, like dog whistles. They might even know a mouse is nearby before you do!

SMELL: Dogs have an INCREDIBLE sense of smell. Some dogs can even be trained to sniff out diseases, such as cancer and diabetes.

Sometimes dogs can tell what you've been up to just by what you smell like!

HOT DOGS

BLOODHOUNDS are champions at tracking scents. Their big ears help fan odors up to their nose.

IRISH WOLFHOUNDS are the tallest breed.

CHIHUAHUAS are the smallest breed.

GERMAN SHEPHERDS are confident and brave. They make good police dogs.

LABRADORS like to run, jump, and swim. They love to play and have fun.

GREYHOUNDS have long legs and are very fast runners.

BASSET HOUNDS are hunters that like to chase rabbits.

SILKY TERRIERS have long flowing hair. They are slightly larger than their Yorkshire terrier cousins.

CHINESE CRESTED dogs have almost no hair at all!

CATS

Some cats are wild and live in the jungle, desert, or rain forest. But domesticated cats make great pets! Just like their wild cousins, they have rough tongues, padded paws, sensitive whiskers, and very sharp claws. Some cats are active and like to chase, pounce, and play, while others like to lay in the sun and sleep.

Pounce:
To swoop down on something suddenly.

Outdoor cats kill billions of birds and small mammals each year in the United States alone. Keep your cats inside. They'll stay safer, and so will other animals!

SUPER SENSES!

VISION: If you look at cats' eyes in bright light, you'll see their pupils get narrow. This lets in less light. But cats can also see well when it's dark. Cells in the back of their eyes reflect light, so at night, cats' eyes may look like they are glowing!

Pupil: The black part in the center of the eye, which is a hole that lets in light.

HEARING: When cats hear noises, their ears turn around. Each ear can focus on a single sound—even in different directions!

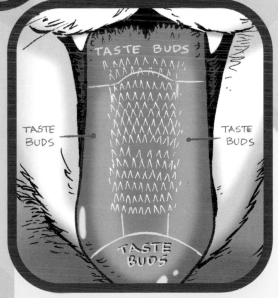

TASTE BUDS

TASTE BUDS

TASTE BUDS

TASTE BUDS

TASTE: Cats can taste sour, bitter, and salty, but not sweet. Their tongues have sharp little spines, which can feel like sandpaper. If a cat licks you, it might tickle!

SMELL: Cats have wet noses. One reason for this is that wet noses pick up smells better than dry ones.

A clowder is a group of cats!

CLOWDER

HOW CAN YOU TELL WHAT A CAT IS FEELING?

When cats are upset, they might start to howl. When they are threatened, they may arch their backs and let out a loud hissing noise.

Cats have flexible spines. This flexibility helps them stretch really long or arch their backs way up high.

Flexible:
Bending easily.

Cats have small floating collarbones. This allows them to fit through tight spaces.

Collarbone: A curved bone that supports the shoulder.

Newborn kittens depend entirely on their mother. But in about a month, they'll start to play with each other. Within a year, they will grow into mature cats!

A kindle is a group of kittens, like the ones in this basket.

Litter: A group of babies born at the same time to one mother.

SIAMESE CATS have short fur. They are very vocal and meow, or "talk," a lot!

TURKISH SWIMMING CATS like to get wet and play!

PERSIAN CATS have long fur. Their long silky coats need a lot of attention.

CALICO CATS have fur with multicolored patches. (Only female cats are colored in this way!)

SCOTTISH FOLD CATS have ears that are folded and flat.

AMERICAN CURL CATS have ears that can curl.

POND LIFE

A pond is a small body of water. It can either be natural or made by humans. Ponds are a freshwater habitat and are home to many animals, such as birds, fish, and insects. All these animals coexist in an ecosystem, feeding off each other and the land for survival.

DUCKS are waterfowl you will frequently see at the pond. When ducklings hatch, they follow their mother in a neat line, one after the other. Ducklings are covered with soft, fuzzy down. This helps them float on the water.

Mother ducks teach ducklings to dabble. They do this by running their beaks across the surface of the water. Grooves in their bills drain the water, so they're left with just the food. These grooves are called lamellae.

Grooves:
Long narrow cuts.

YOU SAY IT!
**Lamellae =
luh-MEL-ee**

LAMELLAE

Many birds breed in one location and spend the winter in another location. We call their journey back and forth a migration. Some travel a short distance. Others travel thousands of miles. Some migrate to find food or to escape the cold. Others migrate for reasons that are not understood. Most waterfowl—including ducks, geese, and swans—are migratory.

When wild **GEESE** migrate, the flock flies in the shape of a V. But the bird in the front gets a lot of wind in its face, which can be tiring. So the geese take turns. After the leader falls back, it will start gliding on airwaves from the new leader.

Flock: A group of animals—usually birds—that eat, live, or travel together.

KINGFISHERS are birds that live near ponds and watch the water from nearby trees. When they see a fish they want to eat, they will swoop down and scoop it right out of the water. Now, THAT'S fast food!

Amphibians are animals that live part-time in water and part-time on land.

FROGS are amphibians that, in general, lay their eggs in the water. They tend to lay many eggs because most will not survive into adulthood. A tadpole, or pollywog, is the larval stage of a frog that hatches from an egg. Tadpoles have gills for breathing underwater, and they eventually grow legs. Their tails begin to shrink, they lose their gills, and they grow lungs for breathing on land. The timetable for these changes varies from one frog species to another, but in the end, the tadpoles that survive grow into frogs!

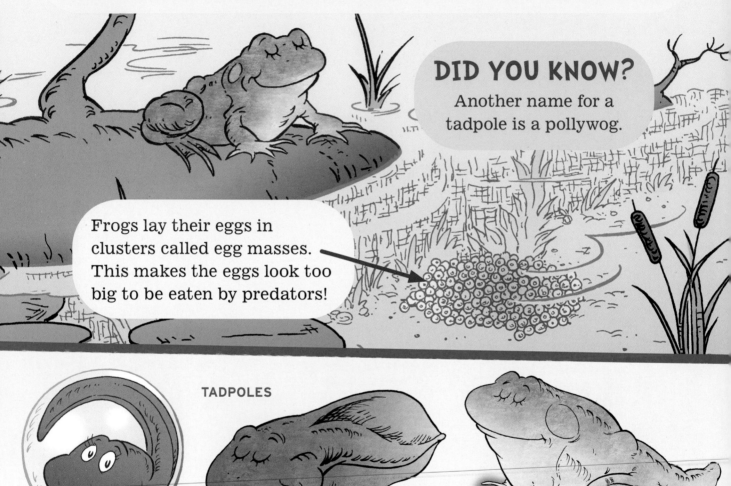

DID YOU KNOW?
Another name for a tadpole is a pollywog.

Frogs lay their eggs in clusters called egg masses. This makes the eggs look too big to be eaten by predators!

TADPOLES

Gills: The breathing organs of some underwater animals.

BULLFROGS are frogs that make loud croaking bellows. The males like to puff up and let loose! This is their way of saying hi to female frogs—and to keep other male frogs away from their territory.

Salamanders, like **NEWTS**, are also amphibians. Some salamanders can lose a limb and regeneratc a new one!

Regenerate: Regrow.

NEWT

TURTLES are reptiles that spend most of their lives in water. Freshwater turtles live in ponds or lakes. They like to lie on rocks or logs and bask in the sun.

Turtle shells are made up of bones covered with scales called scutes that are made of keratin—the same material as your fingernails!

WHAT'S THE DIFFERENCE BETWEEN A FROG AND A TOAD?

Toads are a subset of frogs, generally from the Bufonidae family. However, in popular usage, *frog* is often used to describe frogs with smooth skin, and *toad* is often used to describe frogs with dry, bumpy skin. In addition, toads are generally more land-dwelling than other types of frogs.

Subset: A smaller part of a larger group.

Most **TOADS** need to stay damp, which is one reason they avoid sunlight. If they dry out, they can die!

Pond ecosystems depend on the existence of many different types of insects to thrive. The backswimmer, dragonfly, diving beetle, mayfly, midge, mosquito, water bug, water boatman, water scorpion, and water strider are all insects you would commonly see in a North American pond.

WATER BOATMEN are insects that can breathe underwater—sort of. They take a breath at the surface, then drag the bubble of air underwater to use like a little oxygen tank. When the air bubble is used up, they return to the surface to capture another!

DID YOU KNOW?

MAYFLIES may only live for a total of minutes or hours! They have the shortest life span of all living creatures on Earth.

WATER STRIDERS have long legs covered with tiny hairs that repel moisture and let them stand on the water's surface. To move, they row with their middle legs and steer with their back legs. This helps them avoid becoming prey to fish, frogs, and birds.

Repel: To push away.

FRESHWATER FISH

There are lots of freshwater fish that make their home in North American ponds, lakes, streams, and rivers. As part of these aquatic ecosystems, freshwater fish eat insects, eggs, plants, and even other fish!

SUNFISH swim near the surface of the water.

BULLHEADS and **DARTERS** like to swim down below.

SUNFISH

BULLHEAD

DARTER

PUMPKINSEEDS are a kind of sunfish with very sharp teeth. Their teeth are so sharp they can crush through the shells of freshwater **SNAILS**!

BLUEGILLS and **CRAPPIE** are also sunfish. Bluegills tend to eat insect larvae, and crappie tend to eat algae.

PUMPKINSEED

BLUEGILL

CRAPPIE

SNAIL

Larvae: Young animals that change shape as they grow into adults.

TROPICAL RAIN FOREST ANIMALS

As its name suggests, a rain forest is a forest that receives a lot of rainfall per year. There are two main types of rain forests: tropical and temperate. Tropical rain forests are found near the equator. They are warm and wet all year round, and get the most rain. The Amazon rain forest in South America is a tropical rain forest. It is the largest rain forest in the world and home to 10 percent of Earth's known animal and plant species. Temperate rain forests are located farther away from the equator. They're warm in the summer and cold in the winter, and actually have dry months. The Pacific temperate rain forest of North America runs along the coast from Alaska to Northern California and is the largest temperate rain forest on Earth.

KEEL-BILLED TOUCAN

TROPICAL RAIN FORESTS

A tropical rain forest has four layers:

Fourth layer: **EMERGENT**

Third layer: **CANOPY**

Second layer: **UNDERSTORY**

First layer: **FOREST FLOOR**

DID YOU KNOW?

In a tropical rain forest, over 100 inches of rain can fall each year!

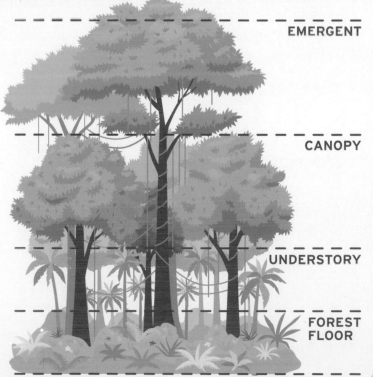

115

EMERGENT: FOURTH LAYER OF THE RAIN FOREST

The top layer of the rain forest is the emergent layer. Emergents are tall trees that poke through the forest canopy. They can be over 150 feet high! Many animals that live in the rain forest will never venture into this layer. But it's a nice place to live or visit for creatures that aren't afraid of heights!

MACAWS are large, colorful parrots that live in the emergent layer of Central and South American rain forests. They can be scarlet, yellow, and blue in color. Unlike most bird species, both the males and females are brightly colored.

Buttress roots

Some emergent trees have roots that grow above the ground! They are called buttress roots. Buttress roots give extra support that helps prevent tall trees from falling down.

CANOPY: THIRD LAYER OF THE RAIN FOREST

The third layer of the rain forest, the canopy, is more crowded than the emergent layer. Here monkeys, tree frogs, and birds eat fruits, nuts, bugs, and the nectar of flowers.

SLOTHS

Algae: Tiny plants without roots, stems, or leaves.

SLOTHS are slow-moving animals native to Central and South American rain forests. During the rainy season, green algae plants grow in the sloths' fur, which helps them blend in with the forest trees.

TROPICAL RAIN FOREST ANIMALS

HOWLER MONKEYS have that name for good reason! They love to howl. Their howls are so loud they can be heard from miles away. These noisy monkeys are commonly found in rain forests in Central and South America.

Believe it or not, **RED-EYED TREE FROGS** can live their entire lives without ever touching the ground! Sticky pads on their toes let them jump and climb without slipping. They spend most of their time near water sources, like ponds and rivers, in rain forests in North, Central, and South America.

Over two hundred kinds of **HUMMINGBIRDS** live in the rain forest canopy! Hummingbirds drink nectar from flowers. They zip around so quickly, they look like insects. While some hummingbird species can only be found in tropical rain forests in South America, other species can be found in much of North America—including the state of Alaska!

Some hummingbirds can beat their wings eighty times a second!

UNDERSTORY: SECOND LAYER OF THE RAIN FOREST

The understory refers to the space below the canopy of trees but above the forest floor. Shrublike vegetation grows in the understory, and animals depend on the humidity in the air to help keep them alive in the tropical heat.

SPIDER MONKEYS use their arms to get around. But they can also hang securely by their tails. That's because their prehensile tails have a very strong grip! Spider monkeys make their home in rain forests in Central and South America.

TROPICAL RAIN FOREST ANIMALS

OCELOTS are cats that live in the rain forest. Like other cats, ocelots have whiskers that help them know which way they are headed. Whiskers also help tell them if it's hot or cold out, and how the wind is blowing. Ocelots are found in North, Central, and South America.

FOREST FLOOR: FIRST LAYER OF THE RAIN FOREST

There is not much sunlight visible from the forest floor. But just because it's dark, doesn't mean it's empty! There are lots of creatures that think the forest floor is the perfect place to live.

JAGUARS are big cats that live in the Amazon rain forest. They are natural predators that like to eat meat, especially capybaras (the largest rodents in the world) and peccaries (boarlike mammals). Jaguars prowl at night to sneak up on their unsuspecting prey. They are also very good climbers!

Jaguars have a rosette pattern on their fur, like leopards. But unlike leopards, jaguars have spots in the middle of their rosettes.

ARMADILLOS are the only mammals in the world with protective armor! Nine-banded armadillos are found in rain forests, grasslands, and deserts in Central and South America and in the southwestern United States. They give birth to four babies at a time. But they won't have a mix of girls and boys. They will have all of one, or all of the other!

There are lots of animals that like to slither and slink in the dead leaves and rot of the forest floor. Watch out for **SNAKES**, **TARANTULAS**, **CENTIPEDES**, and other creepy crawlers!

CENTIPEDE

SNAKE

ANTS

TARANTULA

DEFORESTATION

Tropical rain forests are home to many, many different plants and animals. But rain forests are slowly disappearing, along with the animals that live there. Why? There are different reasons. One is that people are clearing the land for other uses, such as raising cattle, mining, or logging. This is called deforestation. Conservationists are trying to save the rain forests before these plants and animals are lost to us forever.

Conclusion

Earth is home to an incredible variety of marvelous creatures. Whether they are found in the Australian outback or in our own backyards, each animal—from the giant African elephant to the tiny western pygmy blue butterfly—has an important role to play in our world.

As you've seen, animals are special and unique. But not all animals are treated with the respect they deserve. Many are endangered or threatened with extinction. And countless domestic animals need homes. But that doesn't have to be the case. There are lots of things you can do to care for and protect animals—now and when you grow up!

- To start, take good care of your own pets.

- Consider adopting a pet from a shelter or rescue group instead of buying one from a store or breeder.

- Support companies and organizations that put animals first.

- Organize a charity drive to collect items for animals in need.

- Volunteer at a local animal shelter.

Want to work with animals when you grow up? Here are some jobs where you can!

- **Animal welfare workers** include people who work for animal protection groups, like the Humane Society and the American Society for the Prevention of Cruelty to Animals (ASPCA), as well as police departments and animal shelters.

- **Conservationists** act to protect animals, humans, and the environment.

- **Groomers** keep animals clean by washing, brushing, and trimming their hair or fur and nails.

- **Park rangers** help protect animals that live in the wild.

- **Veterinarians** are doctors who provide medical care to animals.

- **Veterinary technicians** assist in veterinary hospitals and clinics to diagnose and treat animals.

- **Wildlife rehabilitators** are experts who can help animals in trouble in the wild.

- **Zoologists** are scientists who study the animal kingdom.

It's up to all of us to preserve our world and the amazing animals that live here. By doing your part, you can help make sure animals not only survive—but thrive—for years and years to come!

We've come to the end.
Now how about that!
Did you learn lots of things
from your old friend, the Cat?

You've read about beasts—
some big and some small.
Is there any way
you'll remember it all?

I hope that you do,
or at least that you try. . . .
And now it is time
for me to say bye!

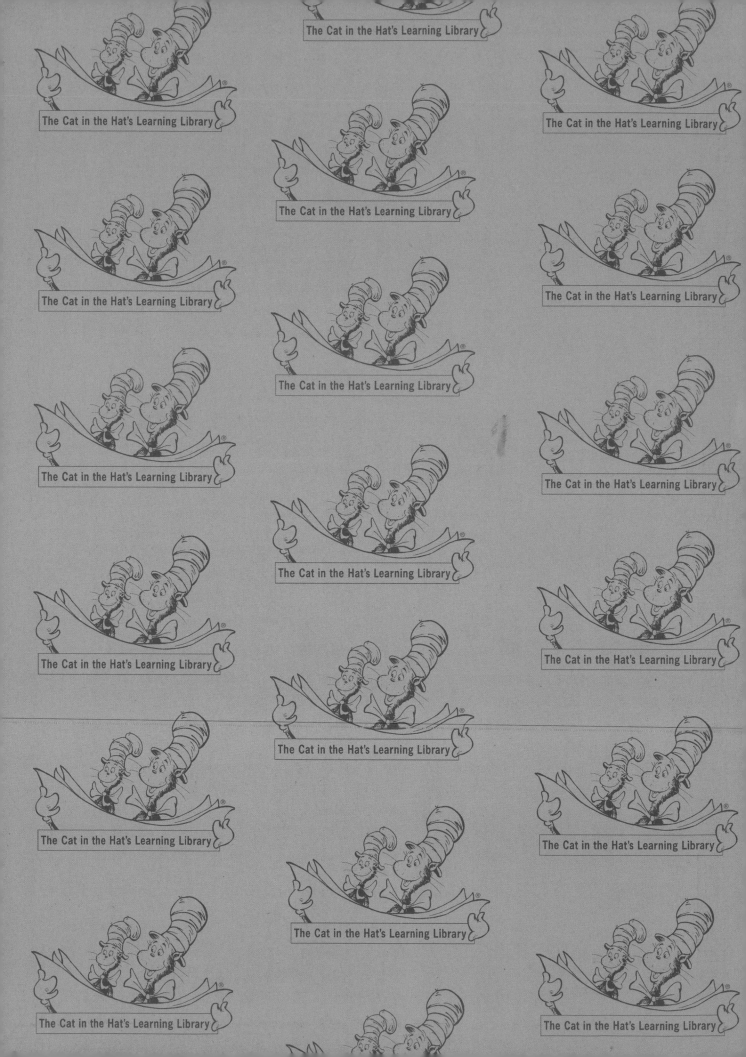